NEVER BALANCE
YOUR CHECKBOOK
ON TUESDAY

NEVER BALANCE YOUR CHECKBOOK ON TUESDAY

*And 300 More Financial Lessons
You Can't Afford Not to Know*

NANCY DUNNAN

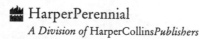

HarperPerennial
A Division of HarperCollins*Publishers*

HarperCollins books may be purchased for educational, business, or sales promotional use. For information, please write to: Special Markets Department, HarperCollins Publishers Inc., 10 East 53rd Street, New York, New York 10022.

FIRST EDITION

Produced by Empire State Packagers

Library of Congress Cataloging-in-Publication Data
Dunnan, Nancy.
    Never balance your checkbook on Tuesday and 300 more financial lessons you can't afford not to know / Nancy Dunnan.
        p.   cm.
    ISBN 0-06-273659-0
    1. Finance, Personal—United States.   2. Saving and Investment—United States.
I. Title.
HG179.08628   1999
332.024—DC21   98-44042

98 99 00 01 02 ❖/RRD 10 9 8 7 6 5 4 3 2 1

Even if you're on the right track,
you'll get run over if you just sit there
WILL ROGERS
1879-1935

ACKNOWLEDGMENTS

The author would like to thank these very special people who contributed their wit, wisdom, and time to this project:

Robert Wilson, my editor at HarperCollins, who conceived and fashioned this series.

Jay Pack, who added to and improved each entry.

Tim Hays, agent and designer for the book.

INTRODUCTION

WILL ROGERS, the quintessential cowboy philosopher and wit, was right on target when he pointed out the importance of getting up and making a move when you see a train barreling down the track.

Perhaps he foresaw the American tendency toward "couch-potato-ism." Indeed, sitting on the track, if it's the right track, works just fine, but only until a better, faster, cleaner train comes along.

So, too, it is with your financial life. Your local bank was a fine place for your savings—until money-market funds came along.

Those old faithful EE bonds were terrific—until zero coupon bonds appeared on the scene.

Social Security was a great concept, too—until 401(k)s were introduced.

New financial products, concepts and strategies do not necessarily negate the validity of older ones—each is entitled to its own track. But the right train is often on another track.

That's why I wrote this book—so you can be on the right track at the right time. You'll find 300 lessons within these pages. Each is simple and easy to follow. Put into action just one a week and you'll find yourself feeling very much in charge of your money. Put one a day into reality and by this time next year you should be richer, wiser, and a whole lot happier about life.

Then, pass this book onto a friend and take joy in putting that person on the right track.

Nancy Dunnan
New York City

ABOUT THE AUTHOR

Nancy Dunnan's many books on money and finance have sold nearly one million copies throughout the United States and Canada. Her down-to-earth guidance to American consumers is consistently prudent, and well-received by her readers.

Ms. Dunnan is a contributor to many consumer magazines, including *Your Money*, *Parents*, and *New Choices*, and is heard on WNYC Public Radio in New York City and nationwide on Business News Network. She may be reached by e-mail at Dunnanbks@aol.com.

Think Smart.

HANDLE YOUR money in the manner in which you'd like your children to handle theirs.

Double Your Money, Double Your Fun.

To QUICKLY calculate how fast your money will double in value, use the RULE OF 72. Divide 72 by the interest rate. If, for example, you're earning 5% in your money market fund, your account will double in 14.4 years. If interest rates jump to 9%, it will take only eight years.

Add Your College Kids to Your Car Insurance.

DON'T BUY them a separate policy. Insuring students as additional drivers on yours is a whole lot cheaper. And beg them to get good grades or else—premiums are less for students with a B averages or better.

Take Advantage of Being 70.

AT THIS point any money earned as income no longer reduces your Social Security benefits, so work as much as you like. (If you are under age 65, $1 is taken away from your benefits for every $2 earned above $9,120 a year. In between ages 65 and 69, $1 is cut for every $3 earned above $14,500.)

Cool It.

SET YOUR air conditioner to keep the room temperature at 78 degrees instead of 72—you'll reduce your energy costs by up to 39%. And, instead of running the AC when no one's home, buy an appliance timer that will turn it on 30 minutes before you walk in the door.

Get Back Your VAT.

VALUE-ADDED TAX, charged on clothing, jewelry, cosmetics and other items in many foreign countries, ranges from 2.9% in Singapore to 20% in Sweden. But it's refundable if you file the right documents. Get the forms when making purchases, follow the directions or ask the salesperson for help. (VAT cannot be reclaimed on hotel rooms, car rentals, meals, drinks.) Need help? Call: Global Refund, 877–714–3893.

— ¢ —

Turn Turning 70½ into a Winner.

ALTHOUGH at this point you must start making minimum distribution withdrawals from just about all retirement accounts, there is one exception: the Roth IRA. You can contribute to a Roth until you die and withdraw money only as you wish.

Save Up to 60% on International Air Fares.

IF YOU have a flexible schedule and can survive with one carry-on bag, sign on to be an air courier. Your checked luggage space will be used for documents and other items shipped by an overnight courier firm. You in turn get to fly for practically nothing. Best source: International Association of Air Travel Couriers: www.courier.org or 561–582–8320.

Make Hay When You Reach 59½.

Now YOU can take out money from your IRA or other qualified retirement plans without being hit with the early withdrawal penalty.

— ¢ —

A Heads Up for Widows and Widowers.

YOU CAN collect Social Security benefits as early as age 60. Others must wait until 62. Even then they don't get as much as if they waited until 65, the point when full benefits kick in.

Beat the Paper Tiger.

WEED OUT those files and keep tax returns just seven years—the IRS has three years in which to audit your return and six years if they think you under-reported income.

CAUTION: If the IRS suspects fraud, there's no statute of limitations, but of course you wouldn't be involved in that. Keep receipts and canceled checks that support your deductions.

Medicate by Mail.

IF YOU TAKE birth control pills, an antidepressant or medication for chronic conditions, buy them from a mail order pharmacy and save a bundle. A good place to start: the American Association of Retired Persons Pharmacy Service, 800–456–7821 or Medi-Mail, 800–922–3444.

Make Two Life and Death Decisions This Month.

FIRST, DRAW up a living will. This document, separate from your regular will, tells your family what medical care you do or do not want to receive if you are terminally ill or unable to state your own wishes. Second, get a health care proxy which authorizes your spouse or another trusted person to decide whether or not you should be kept alive by artificial means if you cannot make that decision.

Skip the Yield and Go for Total Return.

MOST INVESTORS judge a mutual fund by the interest it pays. Big mistake. Use total return instead. A much more thorough way to judge a fund's performance, it measures dividend and/or interest income plus any capital gains. (Capital gains is the profit made when an investment rises in price.)

Stock Up on Stock Options.

THESE GIVE you the option to buy shares of stock in the company you work for from your employer, bypassing a stockbroker. But don't overload on this perk. It's not smart to have more than 15% to 20% of your money tied up in any one company. Even the bluest of the blue chips can turn pale.

Use It or Lose It.

THE MONEY in your Flexible Spending Account, that is. FSAs, offered by many employers, make it possible for employees to pay medical and dependent care expenses with pretax dollars. However, all money left in the account at the end of the year is forfeited.

$TIP: Use up your account by purchasing an extra pair of glasses, getting shots or visiting your dentist.

Buy Your Way into the Best Mutual Funds for Very Little.

MANY TOP funds with high opening minimums ($2,500 and more) let you open an account for far less—if you agree to have a set amount transferred electronically from your checking account into the fund each month. With some funds, it can be as little as $25; most also have lower minimums for IRAs and accounts set up as trusts for children. ASK.

Do Something Lasting.

DRAW UP a durable power of attorney. It designates another person, typically a spouse, adult child or even a lawyer, to take care of your business affairs if you become incapacitated. This person, called the "attorney-in-fact," can sign checks and pay your bills.

$TIP: You can revoke the power at any time.

Stop to Think and Think to Stop.

IF YOU HAVE a stock that's falling in price and you've placed a stop loss order with your broker, then he or she will sell your shares when and if the stock drops to the price you've named. This not only prevents further losses, it also protects any profits you've already earned. Smart step to take if you're going on vacation or out of the country and won't be talking with your broker as much.

Give Life Insurance a Skip.

IF YOU'RE single or married but have no responsibility for taking care of a child, a spouse, elderly parents or a disabled sibling, invest your money instead. The purpose of life insurance is to provide for someone else AFTER you die.

Two Guardian Angels Are Better Than One.

THE PERSON you name in your will as a guardian will raise your child should something happen to both you and your spouse. But if that person is unable to fulfill the position, you want to be the one who picked the alternative guardian. Otherwise, the court, not you, will decide who will take care of your child.

Catch Cramming.

TELEPHONE CRAMMERS will slip small extra charges (of $5 to $30/month) onto phone bills—for things such as voice mail and pagers. Check your statement carefully each month and call your local phone company if there are items you didn't agree to. Be tough. This is a major growing problem.

Pay Down Your Mortgage and Boost Your Frequent Flier Miles.

MAJOR AIRLINES have arrangements with leading lenders through which you get one mile for every dollar you pay each month in mortgage interest. Some grant 1,000 miles for every $10,000 borrowed. Check with the frequent flier programs run by American, TWA, Delta, United and others.

—¢—

Prefer Preferreds.

PREFERRED STOCKS pay significantly higher yields than either the bonds or the common stocks of the same corporation. They are also cheaper to buy than the bonds and more liquid when you go to sell. Look for the initials "pf" next to their listings in the financial pages.

CAUTION: They do not increase in value nor do their dividends rise.

— ¢ —

Do an El Niño Review.

THE RASH OF recent storms and natural disasters prove that no one is 100% safe from nature. So, re-read your homeowner's or renter's insurance policy. Be sure you have "replacement cost" coverage so you'll be paid in full for damaged or destroyed property. Although "cash value" coverage is less expensive, it pays only the market value for items: if your five–year–old refrigerator is worth only one–third of what it costs to buy a new one, you'd have to pick up the other two-thirds.

Lock Up Tight.

OVER 35% OF all burglars enter houses and apartments through windows. Lock yours, clear away surrounding shrubs and trees, and make sure the area is well lit.

Take a Virtual College Tour.

TO REDUCE the cost of visiting colleges with your high schooler, first surf the Web. Most schools have attractive, informational sites. To narrow the number of expensive trips you'll need to pay for even further: order a video from Collegiate Choice, 201–871–0090. It has tours of 300+ colleges.

Buy Solid High-Yielding Stocks on Sale.

BAD NEWS can drive down prices of perfectly sound stocks. If a stock has a good dividend yield there's even less risk.

Beat Savings Account Returns With REITs.

REAL ESTATE INVESTMENT TRUSTS (REITs) are stocks whose companies invest in shopping malls, apartment and office buildings, mortgages, storage centers, continuing care and retirement communities. Yields for the top–rated ones are three times higher than what you can get at your bank. Consider: Weingarten Real Estate, Health and Retirement Properties, and New Plan Reality Trust.

Track Down Money Uncle Sam Owes You.

STILL WAITING for your tax refund? Check on your check by calling the IRS at: 800–829–1040. And, next year, elect to have your refund deposited directly into your bank account; you'll get it much sooner. The appropriate form, #8888, is mailed with the 1040.

Happiness Is Knowing Where Your Money Is.

THINK YOU don't have enough money to save or invest? After checking under the mattress, save: change or dollar bills at the end of the day; cash received for your birthday, graduation or a holiday; lottery winnings; half of your raise; all of a bonus, your tax refund, freelance or moonlighting income, and any inheritance that comes your way.

Check Up on Social Security.

IF YOU'RE WORKING and over age 52, you should already have received at least one "Personal Earnings and Benefit Estimate Statement" from the Social Security Administration. This explains what your retirement benefits will be at ages 62, 65 and 70. But not everyone seems to be on the list. For your copy call: 800–772–1213.

Lease—Again and Again.

CAR LEASING companies like repeat customers, so the second time around, negotiate to waive both the security deposit charges and lease acquisition fees. While you're at it, ask for a better deal. You'll undoubtedly get it, but of course, only if you speak up.

Recession Proof Your Portfolio.

IF YOU THINK the stock market will take a dive, avoid risk-prone investments in emerging markets and go for recession-resistant industries, such as health care, utilities, food, beverages, drugs—all things we must have for everyday living.

Bank on Bad News.

NEGATIVE INFORMATION about a company can be a golden opportunity. Track financially solid companies whose stocks have dropped in price due to one-time events, such as a strike, plant shutdown, bad weather, a product recall, negative publicity, death of the president or CEO. Monitor for several weeks and buy on the first sign of a turnaround.

CAUTION: Don't buy if the company has lost 50% or more of its price within a short period of time.

Don't Supply a "Chop Shop."

THIS IS SLANG for places where stolen cars are stripped in less than 30 minutes so their parts can be sold in the black market. According to the National Insurance Crime Bureau, cars built in 1987 were stolen more frequently than those built in recent years—the older the model, the greater the demand for parts. Lock your older car or truck and install anti-theft devices just as you would in a brand–new Jaguar or Caddy that zigs.

Shop the Internet for Highest Yields.

BANKS ON THE Internet offer better deals because branchless banking is less expensive. Rates on savings accounts and CDs at Security First Network Bank (www.sfnb.com), Atlanta Internet Bank (www.atlantabank.com) and Premium Federal Savings (www.premium.com) are 1% to 2% higher than retail banks.

CAUTION: Scam artists create phony Internet banks with authentic-sounding names. Check with the Federal Deposit Insurance Corp. at www.fdic.gov or 800–934–3312 to make sure a bank is legitimate.

Get Out the Lead.

UNDER FEDERAL law, sellers and landlords must disclose any known lead paint hazards in houses built before 1978. The seller must give the buyer up to ten days to conduct a test. Call: National Lead Information Center, 800–424–LEAD.

Buy Wedding Clothes at Thrift Shops.

YOU'LL FIND beautiful designer dresses, tuxedos and brides-maid's outfits for up to 75% off retail. Another source: dry cleaners. Brides bring their dresses after the wedding and often never pick them up. We won't speculate as to why.

Monitor Medicare Fraud.

IT'S ON THE rise. If you think a provider is trying to swindle you or the system (look for charges for services and medical items you never used and for duplicate billing), call: U.S. Department of Health & Human Services Tip Line: 800–447–8477.

Be a Drip.

BEFORE PAYING a broker's commission to buy a stock, call the company's investor relations department and ask if it has a DIVIDEND REINVESTMENT PLAN and if so, can you also purchase your first share directly from the company. Over 300 companies will let you do so, including Quaker Oats, Walgreen, CSX, Allstate, Campbell Soup, Caterpillar, Whirlpool and Owens–Corning.

Never Get Cash at an Airport Outlet.

AIRPORT EXCHANGE bureaus around the world have outrageously high fees and incredibly poor exchange rates. Hotels aren't much better. Instead, use your ATM card. Most U.S. banks are linked to one of two international networks: Cirrus or Plus. Fees are modest and there are no interest charges.

$TIP: Make one large exchange instead of several smaller ones to further reduce fees.

Know What Car Thieves Know.

ACCORDING TO the National Insurance Crime Bureau, the most commonly stolen cars, last year, were: 1) Honda Accord; 2) Oldsmobile Cutlass Supreme/Ciera; 3) Toyota Camry; 4) Honda Civic; 5) Ford Mustang; 6) Chevrolet Pickup; 7) Toyota Corolla; 8) Cadillac Deville; 9) Chevrolet Caprice; and 10) Jeep Cherokee.

Use a Quote Service.

TO GET THE best life insurance rates, check with Quotesmith (800–556–9393) or SelectQuote (800–343–1985). Then compare with those offered by your insurance agent.

– ¢ –

Leave Your Social Security Card at Home.

IF YOUR PURSE or wallet is stolen, the thief can use your number for all kinds of outrageous criminal schemes.

41

Hold On Tight.

UNDER THE NEW tax act, if you're in the 28% tax bracket you'll pay only 20% in capital gains tax when you sell investments held more than 12 months. But, sell before 12 months and you'll be hit with a 28% tax. Investors in the 15% bracket get an even better deal—they pay just 10% in capital gains for stocks held 12 months. In the year 2001, they will pay 8% on stocks you own five years or more.

— ¢ —

Land the House You Would Die For.

TO BEAT OUT the competition, come up with a larger down payment, or all cash. Then, sweeten the deal by offering to let the seller remain in the house for free for 30 to 60 days. Follow up by writing the seller saying how much you love the house. Even the toughest negotiators go soft if they think their house will be lived in by someone who likes it as much as they do.

Wear Tight Clothes When Shopping.

YOU'LL FEEL LESS hungry at the grocery store. And, when bargain hunting at thrift shops without a dressing room, you can try on clothes over your outfit, dab smack in the center aisle, in front of God and everyone.

Play the Merger Game.

MERGERS BOOST stock prices. To be in on the ground floor, look for: 1) ripe companies with rapid growth (banks, brokerage firms, radio and TV broadcasting companies and electric utilities, regional telephone companies); 2) companies owned by families who want to sell out; 3) companies owned by someone older or in poor health.

Safeguard Your Wheels.

A VEHICLE IS stolen every 21 seconds, so have the identification number of your car or SUV etched on the window. This not only puts off thieves, it also makes it easier for the police to trace your car if it's stolen.

$TIP: Many local police stations will do this for free, although they rarely advertise the fact.

Count Your (ATM) Numbers.

OVERSEAS ATM machines use four–digit personal identification numbers (PINs). If yours is five or six digits, ask for it to be reduced to four before leaving the country.

Count Your (ATM) Letters.

OVERSEAS ATM machines often have numeric keypads. If you have an alphabetical PIN, figure out its numerical equivalent and memorize those numbers before leaving the country.

Fly High at 62.

THIS IS THE AGE at which most airlines give travelers a 10% discount on published fares. It's also when senior coupon books are available—for a flat fee, you buy a booklet of four or eight coupons, good for a year, which you exchange for one-way tickets to wherever the airline flies. These coupons, available only for the 62+ crowd, give the best rates on longer flights, so don't waste them on short commuter hops.

— ¢ —

Buy the Stock Of the Company Being Taken Over.

YOU'RE MORE LIKELY to make money with this company than with the one doing the buying. The latter has to lay out a lot of cash, reducing share value. It may even have to borrow heavily, thus creating new debt and ongoing interest payments.

— ¢ —

Turn Anniversaries into Money.

HOTELS, RESTAURANTS, airlines, cruises, and tour packagers celebrate their companies' major anniversaries by offering special deals and discounts to clients and customers. Watch for ads. THE FLIP SIDE: If it's your wedding anniversary or birthday, tell everyone in the travel and restaurant business—you'll land discounts, if not freebies.

Tell the Truth About Your Age.

IF YOU'VE SHAVED a few years from your age, fess up. Company health and retirement benefits as well as Social Security checks are directly linked to age, with the last five years of work increasing retirement benefits by a significant amount. Take your birth certificate to your firm's benefits officer; if you're self–employed, get in touch with your local Social Security office. If you still insist on pretending, do so knowing you'll miss out on what's your due.

Buy Flood Insurance.

MORE THAN 25% of flood claims come from areas not prone to them—hurricanes, high tides and other disasters often affect inland areas. Get coverage if you live near a coast, river, lake, creek, golf course pond or a low–lying area. Not all insurance companies sell flood coverage. For the name of one that does, get in touch with FEMA at 800–427–4661.

Jump Start Your Child's Savings.

IF YOUR KID has earned income, he can open a regular or a Roth IRA; earnings in both grow tax-free. The maximum contribution for either is $2,000 a year.

$TIP: If your child spent his summer earnings on concert tickets and pizza, you or his grandparents can gift him the IRA contribution just as long as there's official documentation that he earned the amount of the contribution.

Do a Quick Read.

PROBABLY THE ONLY person that bothers to read a mutual fund's annual report from cover to cover is the fund manager. There's no need for you to follow suit. However, before you invest, read: 1) the letter to shareholders to learn management's investment philosophy; 2) the financial statement describing the fund's turnover rate, expenses and capital distributions; and 3) the list of portfolio holdings so you'll know what stocks, bonds and Treasuries it owns.

Put Off Paying Student Loans.

IF YOU'RE UNEMPLOYED, you can defer payment on Stafford, SLS, Plus, consolidation loans and recent Perkins loans for up to three years. But you must be seriously looking for work and willing to name companies where you've applied for a job.

Buy a Beach House in January.

AND A SKI CHALET IN August. When it comes to vacation homes, you'll save 10% to 20% by wheeling and dealing off–season or after a long siege of bad weather.

Move On After a Bank Merger.

THEY OFTEN RESULT in higher fees, lower deposit rates and less personalized service. A recent Federal Reserve Board study found that large multistate banks tend to charge more fees than single state based banks, so shop around for the best deals. Or, join a credit union where you'll earn 1 to 2½% more on savings and pay considerably less on loans. Call: Credit Union National at 800–356–9655.

Hang On to Home Improvement Records.

ALTHOUGH THERE'S now a $250,000 capital gains exclusion for profits on a home sale ($500,000 for a couple filing jointly), you might sell your house for a fortune and exceed these caps. You'll need those records for reducing your liability.

— ¢ —

Calculate Credit Card Creep.

THE INTEREST RATE on many cards is now above 20% if you miss two payments within a six–month period. **$TIP:** This bad news is always buried in a footnote in very small print.

Take Advantage of Being a Working Mom.

IF YOU HAVE preschool-age children and you're holding a job, you can defer paying back Stafford, SLS and Perkins college loans for up to one year; ditto if you're a working mother earning no more than $1 above the federal minimum wage. If you're on parental leave, caring for a newborn or newly adopted child, some loans can be deferred for up to six months.

Be House-Rich, House-Proud and Cash-Full.

IF YOU'RE A homeowner at least 62 years old, you can get equity out of your primary residence while still living in it with a "reverse mortgage." You may get money in a lump sum or periodically. Use a reliable lender, such as FHA's HOME EQUITY CONVERSION, for homes worth less than $170,362, FANNY MAE HOMEKEEPER for homes up to $227,150. Find information about private lenders at NATIONAL CENTER FOR HOME EQUITY CONVERSION at: www.reverse.org, or call 612–953–4474.

Switch Mutual Funds Without Getting Taxed.

YOU SHOULD change funds when there's a significant change in the market or your personal life. You won't pay taxes on the change in your 401(k)until you withdraw money from the plan.

— ¢ —

Lower Funeral Expenses.

IF YOU'RE THE spouse of a veteran, check with the Veterans Administration Office regarding a burial allowance or even free internment: 800–827–1000.

Never Use Your Credit Card for Cash Advances Overseas.

YOU'LL BE charged interest the minute you make a withdrawal. Be smart: use your ATM card—the cash comes interest free.

— ¢ —

Always Charge Overseas Purchases.

BECAUSE credit card issuers give very favorable wholesale exchange rates to users abroad, you get about 5% more for your dollar than if you use local currency or travelers checks. Use your card to pay for hotels, restaurants, clothing, presents.

Merge Love and Student Loans with Your Eyes Wide Open.

IF YOU'RE MARRIED, you can consolidate your college loans, but both of you then must agree to repay the ENTIRE loan if you divorce. And, if one of you dies, the other is responsible for any remaining consolidated loan. Unless yours is a marriage made in heaven, keep college loans separate.

Wearing A Military Uniform Pays.

WHILE YOU'RE on active duty, you can defer payments on Stafford, SLS, consolidation or PLUS college loans. If you're in an area of hostility or are in imminent physical danger, the Defense Department will actually repay up to half of your Perkins student loan.

— ¢ —

Buy Ski Boots In August.

OR SEPTEMBER...as well as ice skates, parkas, snowshoes and skis. You'll save up to 25%.

Fix Up Your House First and Then Fix Your Insurance.

IF YOU ADD $5,000 worth of work to your house, or increase its value by 5%, you need to buy additional coverage.

$TIP: Because building costs go up every year, make sure your policy has a 2% to 4% inflation protection clause.

Fight Back and Hang Tough.

THERE'S NO SUCH thing as an ironclad "company policy." This phrase is used from Wall Street to Main Street to discourage consumers from making official complaints, from suing, or asking for refunds or replacement items. Don't cave in. Instead, confront management, not the telephone operator or clerk: "That policy is not in writing." "I wasn't told that at the time of purchase." "That's disgraceful—I'm going to contact the Better Business Bureau." "I'm taking notes on our conversation." Then there's the always effective: "I'll have my lawyer get in touch with you." Document all conversations.

Help Mom and Dad.

IF YOUR ELDERLY parents are forgetting to pay bills or filing their tax returns late or not at all, it's time to ask how you can help them manage day–to–day stuff. Most likely they'll be very relieved. If you live far away, you can find a local community service that will fill in for you through Eldercare Locator, 800–677–1166, or click on: aoa.dhhs.gov.

Don't Be a Clinging Vine.

PLANTS THAT attach themselves to the walls of your house may look lovely but they are impossible to remove without damaging the structure. They also prevent you from seeing those areas that need repair and provide a perfectly logical excuse for not painting. In the long run, you'll suffer from creeping expenses. Settle for a trellis.

— ¢ —

Buy Secondhand Sports Equipment for Beginners.

YOU'LL SAVE UP to 80% over new golf clubs, tennis racquets, and SCUBA gear. Then, if you or your kids get hooked, move up to the high–end stuff. SOURCES: garage sales, neighbors, school coaches (they know which kids have dropped the sport or graduated) and gyms where people often leave equipment when they move on.

Shop the Outlets.

YOU'LL SAVE an average of 30% off retail on designer brand items. But go with a list and remember—shopping is still shopping and spending is still spending. Many are located in vacation areas and have become popular tourist destinations in and of themselves. If you're traveling and want to locate the nearest outlet (there are over 500 outlet malls all around the US), call 800–OUTLET–2 or click on www.outletbound.com.

Use Unconventional Means to Buy a Conventional House.

IF YOUR CREDIT history is tarnished or your income is low, you may qualify for a FHA or VA mortgage. Conventional loans require that mortgage payments, property taxes and home-owner's insurance combined not be more than 28% of gross income and those payments, plus any other debt, not be more than 36% of your gross income—known as the 28/36 ratio. The less conventional FHA ratio is 29/41; the VA is more lenient: 41/41.

Shop with the Gang.

GET A BUSLOAD of friends or neighbors together for a trip to an outlet mall. Then, call the mall's manager and tell him when 20 of your nearest and dearest will be arriving. Very likely you'll be greeted personally, given discount coupon books, taken to a fashion show and maybe treated to lunch or tea.

Spruce Up Your Car.

CHANGE YOUR transmission oil and have the filters cleaned every 30,000 miles. Every three years, flush the cooling system to prevent corrosion. A car in good mechanical condition uses up to 15% less gas than an old wreck.

Keep It to Yourself.

NEVER GIVE out your credit card number except to a company you know or trust. Ditto on your mother's maiden name, your bank PIN number or your Internet password.

Protect Yourself from Internet Scams.

IT'S BUYER beware just as it is anywhere else. Never ever disclose your Social Security number and steer clear of businesses that don't post their street address and phone number. Ask for written information if you have any doubts and make sure the Web site has a security mode that encrypts credit card numbers. The Better Business Bureau, at: www.bbbonline.org, certifies Web businesses that meet its standards. Keep up to date about rip-offs by reading the Federal Trade Commission's consumer alerts at: www.ftc.gov.

Don't Shrink the Kids.

INSTEAD, buy clothes one size too large. Kids grow fast and even prewashed items shrink. Pick out baby-style dresses without a definite waistline for your daughter. She'll be able to wear them much longer. (This works for moms, too.)

— ¢ —

Be Discreet with Technology.

NEVER SEND an e-mail you'd be embarrassed to see on the office bulletin board or in your local newspaper. Likewise, don't leave any confidences on a voice mail.

Stop Junk Mail and Save a Tree.

AMERICANS GET two million tons of junk mail a year. To de-list your name, call the Direct Marketing Association's Mail Preference Service at 212–768–7277. This will end the barrage of catalogs tempting you to buy things you don't need.

— ¢ —

Teach and Be Forgiven.

STUDENT LOANS may be canceled or deferred if you teach low income or disabled students, or work in a field designated by the Department of Education as a "teacher shortage area."

Beware of Phony IRS Agents.

IMPOSTERS ABOUND, swindling thousands of dollars from unsuspecting Americans. To avoid being taken, keep in mind that: 1) you must be notified of an IRS audit by letter, not by phone; 2) all IRS employees carry IDs; and 3) they never ask that checks be made out to them personally.

Rent Infrequent Items.

IF YOU USE something only now and then, such as a power tool, party tables, rug shampooing machines, floor waxers, holiday costumes, bikes, even a car, rent, don't buy. Better yet, go in together with neighbors and colleagues. Duplication is a waste of money. The only item that qualifies for onetime use is your wedding dress.

Buy an Iced Door.

A REFRIGERATOR that dispenses ice from the outside door means you and the kids won't keep opening and closing it for cubes. When you do, the unit burns up more energy, benefiting only your local electric utility company.

Tear First, Toss Second.

SHRED YOUR BANK statements, credit-card receipts, airline ticket stubs, preapproved credit card offers. Theft of documents from trash is the fastest growing fraud of the decade.

Get a Free Presidential Portrait.

A COLOR PHOTOGRAPH of the President is yours if you send your name and address to: Office of Correspondence, Room 94, The White House, Washington, DC 20500. If you're not a friend of Bill's, you can order one of the First Lady, Vice President Al Gore, Tipper Gore or the completely apolitical Socks, the First Cat. That's one less decorating item you'll need to spend money on.

Set Up a "Buyer's Remorse" Account.

IF YOU TRY ON a suit but don't buy it, return an unused appliance, send back shoes ordered from a catalog, or are otherwise prudent, put the price of each item into this special savings account. Watch it grow. Every once in a while, use it to treat yourself or your family to something extra special.

Go for an Attractive Showroom Model.

WHEN SHOPPING for large appliances, bikes, cars and furniture, ask if the floor model can be purchased at a reduced price. You'll save anywhere from 10% to 50%. But skip this lesson if scratches and dents drive you crazy, unless you're handy at fixing things.

Spell It Out.

WHEN YOU HAVE the task of writing a check to the IRS, spell out in full the words Internal Revenue Service. The initials IRS are easily altered by criminals. Always add your Social Security number to your check and specify exactly what the payment is for—estimated taxes, late charges, your 1040, etc.—with the tax year.

Carry a List of Clothing Sizes.

THEN WHEN you spot a great bargain, you'll know if it will actually fit someone in your family. As Henny Youngman said: "It's easy to tell when you've got a bargain; it doesn't fit."

−¢−

Move on a Weekday.

FEES ARE AS much as 50% higher on weekends. Pack everything yourself and save 10% to 20%.

Never Lend Uncle Sam a Penny.

IF YOU'RE GETTING a tax refund, that means you're making an interest-free loan to the U.S. Treasury by having too much withheld from your paycheck. Adjust your withholding. Get the W-4 worksheet from your company's personnel office so that it matches what you owe and no more.

See the Light.

HERE'S A BRIGHT idea. Those odd-shaped lightbulbs called CFLs (compact fluorescent lightbulbs) use about $17 of electricity over their lifetime; a 75-watt incandescent will use $63 worth. And, because CFLs last longer you don't have to buy as many.

Get Out Your Sweaters.

FOR EACH DEGREE you lower your thermostat setting, you reduce your fuel bill by 2%.

Skip First–Run Films.

ALL BUT THE really big blockbusters are out on video within three months, sometimes earlier. The cost of a movie in New York City is $8.50 versus a rental fee of $4, on average. If you watch with three buddies you'll have enough left over to buy a take-out dinner—all for less than the cost of the movie alone. Many public libraries also have videos, books on tape and CDs.

Remember Your Net Worth.

USE IT TO DETERMINE the appropriate risk level for all your investments. If your net worth is over $1 million, buy an umbrella liability insurance policy to protect your assets in the event you're sued. Just $300 gets you $1 million in coverage.

Damper Down.

THE U.S. DEPARTMENT of Energy estimates that an open damper in a 48-inch square fireplace allows as much as 8% of a home's heat to go right up and out the chimney.

Pick Your Travel Tour Carefully.

SOME OPERATORS are fly-by-nights; others just klutsy. Use a tour company that belongs to the U.S. Tour Operators Association. It requires members to have $1 million in liability insurance. Then if the operator goes under, you'll get back your money. The National Tour Association has a similar plan.

Move Money Around.

THE YEAR BEFORE your child goes off to college is the year in which you want to show the lowest income possible so you can qualify for the greatest amount of financial aid.

File Early for College Financial Aid.

THE SOONER YOU get started, the greater your chances are for getting a financial aid package with a higher ratio of grant dollars (money you don't have to repay) to loan dollars—which obviously you do have to repay. The reason: many colleges, especially smaller, less well-endowed ones, give out grants on a first-come, first-served basis. Call the school to see how soon you can begin the process.

Take In a Boarder.

COLLEGE STUDENTS often need places to stay. Check references first and then put everything in writing. If you don't know the student, rent for one semester and renew your agreement if it works out. In exchange for a reduced rent, the boarder may be willing to baby-sit, cook, clean. Visiting college professors are also likely candidates, but don't expect them to do household stuff. Tell area colleges that you have a spare room.

Beware Bogus "Scholarship Search" Scams.

THIS LATEST SCAM, which is duping more than 350,000 people a year, assures students free scholarship money in exchange for an up-front fee. Signs of a phony deal: you're told the scholarship is guaranteed or your money back (no scholarship is guaranteed) or that the scholarship will cost you money (no scholarship or grant will cost you money). Another ploy: give us your credit card or bank account number to hold this scholarship. REALLY!

Think Small.

A FEDERAL RESERVE BANK of New York survey of 499 bank mergers found that larger merged banks pay 4.1% less on CDs and 3.3% less on money market accounts than smaller banks.

Get a Call Back.

IF YOU SEE something you like at a garage sale, but it's too pricey, leave your name, phone number and the amount you're willing to pay for the item. If it isn't sold by the end of the sale, ask the seller to let you know.

Inspect First and Buy Later.

A GOOD HOME inspector will turn up flaws that you should know about before buying a house. If the problems are really serious, make sure that you have a right to withdraw your bid on the house and end the deal. **$TIP:** Never ask the seller's broker for the name of an inspector, an obvious conflict. To find one who will be on your side, call the American Society of Home Inspectors, 800–743–ASHI.

Buy New Stocks After They're a Month Old.

IPOs (INITIAL PUBLIC OFFERINGS) very often climb in price when they first go public; then, several weeks later, decline. That's the time to add them to your portfolio, but only if earnings appear to be strong and sales are headed up.

Think Twice About Early Admission.

IT MAY DECREASE the amount of financial aid your child receives because the college, knowing it's at the top of your child's wish list, figures you're willing to pay more to send your high schooler to his/her number one choice.

Financial Solution for the Timid but Smart.

A MUTUAL FUND 100% invested in U.S. Treasuries is as safe as you can get. Interest earned is free of state and local taxes.

Finance Your Car.

BUT ONLY WHEN auto loan rates are lower than what you're making on your savings or investments. Otherwise, pay cash.

— ¢ —

Put the Spin on Spin-offs.

THESE STOCKS generally go up in price after they're sold by their parent companies because they are run by experienced managers who know the business as well as how to cut costs. And 14% of spin-offs later become takeover targets, further boosting the price of their stock.

Be a Credit Union Crossover.

THE AVERAGE number of monthly ATM visits made by Americans is 15; at $1.50 per visit that adds up to $270/year. If you use an ATM machine owned by a bank other than yours, you'll also be hit with a noncustomer surcharge averaging $1.13.

SOLUTION: Head for a credit union: only 16% impose surcharges versus 63% of banks. For a directory of no-fee credit union ATM machines, click on www.cuna.org or call 800–356–9655.

Don't Tow the Car to Any Old Shop.

IF YOU HAVE an accident, call your auto insurer for repair shop recommendations. Then ask the insurance company to send an adjuster to inspect the car at the shop before issuing a check. This gives you leverage to get a really good job.

— ¢ —

Pretend You're in Debt.

ONCE YOU'VE paid off a loan, such as your mortgage, student or car loan, save at least half that amount. You haven't been starving without it, nor will you now.

Review Your Money Market Fund Yield Every Quarter.

TOP-YIELDING ONES often lose their lead rankings because their high interest rates are due to management waiving some or all of the fund's expenses. When the high yields bring in enough money, fund managers tend to start including expenses, so yields drop. **$TIP:** Don't hesitate to switch to a higher–yielding fund—selling money market shares is not taxable because the net value of each is always $1.

Dress for Dress Rehearsals.

TICKETS TO concerts and plays can be outrageously expensive. Find out when the rehearsals are being held; tickets are often half-price or even free, especially for students.

— ¢ —

Chart the Top Ten.

THE LEADING stocks and mutual funds are listed weekly in major newspapers. A newcomer to the leaders' list signals a buying opportunity.

Ask Your Boss for Tax-Free Benefits.

A RAISE IN pay, although very nice, is fully taxable to you. Most fringe benefits, however, are tax free for you and tax deductible for your employer. Ask for: free parking, bus or subway pass, child care assistance, discounts at local stores, college tuition for you or for your children.

Steer Clear of Airport Car Rentals.

SPECIAL CHARGES imposed on rental companies for the use of prime space wind up adding 15% to 20% to the rates you pay. Find an agency away from the airport, on the highway or, in most cities, downtown. Many will let you return the car to the airport location at no extra charge.

Never Move in the Summer.

JUNE, JULY AND AUGUST are the busiest and most expensive months in which to move. Determine your mover's slow time.

Challenge Your Property Tax.

QUESTION YOUR assessment through official channels and you may be one of thousands of Americans whose real estate taxes are reduced by 10% or more. Call your local assessor's office for details and a time schedule. Most localities allow appeals 60 to 90 days after tax bills are mailed.

Read the Small Print.

LEAFLETS STUCK in your credit card statements contain information about increases in annual fees, charges for those who pay promptly (unbelievable, isn't it?), outrageous increases in annual interest rates for late payments or for going over your credit limits. Call the issuer to protest vigorously; threaten to switch credit cards and do if you don't get results.

Skip the Camera and Guidebook.

THIEVES AND pickpockets will spot you a mile away as a tourist. Instead, put travel items in an ordinary tote. A plastic bag from a local grocery or drug store, while not chic, is even better.

Adjust Your Life Insurance.

KEY EVENTS THAT signal more coverage is called for: birth of a baby, home purchase, a higher risk type of job. Events that signal less coverage is needed: a child's college graduation, divorce, retirement, death of a spouse or beneficiary.

Know What Burglars Like and Don't Give It to Them.

THE SMART ones look for cartons waiting for garbage pickup, a telltale sign that you've purchased a large appliance, TV, VCR. They also love open garage doors, indicating whether or not you've left home, and huge piles of newspapers announcing that you've gone fishing.

Know What Burglars Don't Like and Give It to Them.

THEY HATE ACTIVITY—clothes drying on the line, water sprinklers sprinkling, radios playing, lights glowing, driveway gravel crunching and, of course, visible alarm systems.

— ¢ —

Bombproof Your Portfolio.

INVEST IN stocks that have raised dividends at an annual rate of 10% over ten years. Examples: Travelers Group, Johnson & Johnson, Merck. Ask your broker for others.

Go for a High Five.

TO BE ADEQUATELY diversified, begin by investing in five stocks and aim to eventually own ten. Studies indicate that you can get most of the benefits of diversification with just eight or ten companies.

$TIP: Your five stocks absolutely must be in five different industries. Then, if one has a rough patch, you'll be protected by the other four.

Invest the Same in All Five Stocks.

PUT 20% IN each; if you own eight, it's 12.5% in each; with ten stocks, 10% in each. This no-brainer approach makes investing simple and monitoring results a snap.

— ¢ —

Commute Before Committing.

TEST OUT THE trip to/from work before buying a new house or condo. Make the journey at the same time of day as if you were living in the area. Sellers inevitably shorten the actual commute time when negotiating in their wish to close the deal.

Scan for Errors.

A FEDERAL TRADE COMMISSION study of 17,000 items in 300 stores found that nearly 10% of scanned prices in grocery stores were wrong. Sale items were at the top of the list. Don't be too shy to compare your receipt with the actual prices at the checkout counter. The same rule applies to restaurant checks: make sure you ordered what the waiter charged you for. And, always challenge a total if you know it's wrong.

Insurance Solution for the Timid but Smart.

AN UMBRELLA policy, which is extra personal liability coverage, protects your assets in case a huge lawsuit is filed against you because of physical injury, libel, even mental anguish. In today's litigious society, million-dollar damage awards may be peanuts, but if you can't pay, your assets can be seized and/or your salary garnisheed. It's worth the $150 to $350 a year for a $1 million umbrella.

Protect Your Wallet.

IF IT'S STOLEN, your life becomes an open book, with the thief and all his or her pals knowing where you live, where you work, where you bank and more. Make a record of everything you have in your wallet. Photocopy the front and back of all cards and then add the appropriate toll-free service numbers to each. Keep copies of the list at home and at work. Then if you need to report stolen or lost cards, you can do so immediately.

If It Is Stolen.

REPORT THE THEFT to your credit card companies and banks immediately. Stolen cards are generally used within a matter of hours. If blank checks were taken, close your checking account and open a new one, even if the bank says it won't honor the missing checks. Mistakes happen. Tell the police and get a file report number. Your insurance company will want this as documentation for your claim.

Fly Right and You'll Fly Cheap.

MAJOR AIRLINES typically have lower fares on flights leaving on Tuesday, Wednesday and Thursday. Saturday night stayovers also cut the price. With some carriers, the time of day makes a big difference. Be willing to book a stopover—nonstop flights usually cost more.

$TIP: Tell your agent or the reservationist that you're willing to fly anytime to land the best deal.

Think Nearly New, Not Old and Used.

A NEW CAR becomes used the second it leaves the dealer's lot. The same is true of clothes, furs, jewelry, toys, sports equipment. The more nearly new items you buy the more you'll save. Calculate how much and put that amount in a special fund. Use it for a vacation, a night on the town, or a day at a health club or spa.

Know When to Sell a Stock.

IF YOU BOUGHT it for growth, hold it as long as the company's earnings continue to rise steadily. If profits slow down, find out why and sell, unless you're confident they will increase within six months to a year. If you bought the stock for income, keep it as long as the company is financially solid, and as long as earnings are rising by more than 5% annually and exceeding the dividend by at least 10%. If earnings are flat and/or the firm's creditworthiness is downgraded, sell.

Insure Two Lives.

FIRST-TO-DIE LIFE insurance covers both husband and wife but pays off when the first one dies. This lets the surviving spouse keep his/her standard of living even if medical costs and final illness expenses of the deceased have drained their savings. It's expensive, so buy only if you don't have adequate coverage through other types of insurance or trusts.

Avoid Income.

IT'S HARD TO BELIEVE, but dividend and interest income is a plus for the IRS. That's because these two types of income are taxed at ordinary rates, which can be as high as 39.6%. But investments held at least 12 months are taxed at just 20%. So, if you're in a high tax bracket think twice about loading up on bank CDs, Ginnie Maes, high-yielding corporate bonds and money market accounts.

Build Your Frequent Flier Miles.

PAY FOR major expenses and big ticket items with an airline affinity card, including college tuition. Many schools now accept plastic.

— ¢ —

Boot Up but Pay Less.

IF YOU don't need this week's software or hardware on your computer, or you just need a backup machine, buy a used or discontinued model. Nearly all can be upgraded and will work with most peripherals. Try: Boston Computer Exchange, 800–262–6399 or Onsale at: www.onsale.com.

Prepare Ahead of Time for a Paid Leave.

MORE AND MORE employers are asking employees to pay back their salary and health insurance—if they don't go back to work for the company. This should be a heads up, particularly for women who take a maternity leave and then decide to be stay–at–home moms.

$TIP: Read the fine print of any agreement and discuss it with your lawyer before signing.

Climb the Treasury Ladder to Safety.

To PROTECT against inflation or changing interest rates, ladder Treasury notes—buy them to come due at staggered intervals, two, three, four and five years. Then you'll have money available periodically which you can reinvest in additional Treasuries, move to stocks or bonds or use to buy bank CDs. The minimum purchase for two– and three–year T notes is $5,000; for longer maturities, $1,000. **$TIP:** Buy through your area's Federal Reserve Bank or branch at no charge.

Know What's Inside.

YOUR SAFE DEPOSIT BOX, that is. Most people don't visit their box even once a year. Keep a list of the contents as well as copies of all stored documents at home or in your office. The box should contain: birth and death certificates, marriage license, divorce papers, citizenship and adoption papers, deeds, automobile titles, copies of trusts and copies of your latest will.

Don't Give Out Your Address.

WHEN GETTING an estimate for home repairs, installations, landscaping, swimming pool services, tree spraying or carpet cleaning...get the quote first, then reveal your location. Contractors and workers often hike prices when they hear a fashionable address. And, be sure to get several bids, one of which should be from someone who does not live in the neighborhood.

Retire in a Tax Haven.

IF YOU HAVE income above and beyond Social Security, aim to wind up in a state that has no personal income tax: Alaska, Florida, Nevada, South Dakota, Texas, Washington and Wyoming. Although New Hampshire and Tennessee do not have a personal income tax, they insist you pay taxes on dividends and income.

Don't Lose Your Money.

WHEN MAKING an electronic transfer of assets from one institution to another, transfer everything. Partial switching can create problems and errors. If you absolutely must transfer only some assets, give written instructions to both the new and the old institutions and keep a copy. Spell out in detail what goes and what stays.

Turn Down Interest Payments.

ONE WAY TO boost your return is to buy CDs in which the interest rate is reinvested and not paid out until the certificate comes due. This gives you the big advantage of compound interest. Example: a one-year CD at 4.5% that does not mail you the interest until maturity actually yields 4.75% on the initial amount invested.

Show Off Your Credentials.

TO REDUCE car rental rates, roll out your AARP or AAA membership number, your business card, airline frequent flier memberships, newspaper ad, your marriage license if you're newlyweds, proof of your wedding date if you're going on an anniversary trip, even school connections. Car rental agencies give different discounts for different affiliations at different times.

Smaller Is Better.
Less _Is_ More.

MOVING TO A smaller house or apartment means many good things: lower utility bills, less lawn to mow, fewer weeds, shorter sidewalks and driveways to shovel, reduced property taxes, lower insurance costs, less space to decorate and, of course, less to dust, polish and vacuum.

Watch for People Bearing Large Purses and Tote Bags at Your Garage Sale.

THESE ARE standard operating uniforms for no–goodniks. They sneak little items into both, without paying for them. Price tag switching is another ploy.

$TIP: Station helpers at each table and ask browsers to check their bags.

Get That Raise.

SHOW UP EARLY, leave late, bring in new business, save the company money, help your boss look good, dress neat, be mannerly but don't suck up to management. Then, when you get an increase (or a bonus), save at least one-third of it in your money market fund. You were living without it, so why not continue to do so.

Never Schedule Your Move for the Day After Closing On a House.

WHEN IT COMES to buying real estate, delays are incredibly commonplace. It might even be you who needs the extra time—because of unexpected fees, inability to get a certified check in time, even illness—yours or your lawyers. Give yourself a week's leeway.

Let Your Parents Pay.

THEIR HEALTH CARE costs, that is. After they go through their own savings, then Medicaid will take care of their expenses. But if you spend your money, Medicaid will neither give you credit nor step up to the plate. In other words, any money you spend out of pocket simply delays their eligibility for Medicaid.

Limit Your Child's Savings.

SEEMS RIDICULOUS, but the more a student saves, the less financial aid he's likely to get. That because colleges assume that 35% of all financial assets in a child's name is available to pay for tuition versus 6% of money in the parents' names. For example: $10,000 saved in Junior's name will reduce college financial aid by $3,500. The same ten grand in the parents' names will reduce aid by only $600.

Buy Small, Save Big.

LOOK FOR TRIAL sizes of new health and beauty products, coffee, tea and condiments. Introductory prices are always low; even lower if you have a coupon.

Remember You're a Woman (If You Are).

WOMEN LIVE FIVE to seven years longer than men and are more apt to work in jobs not offering pensions. So save early and often. Men, of course, should follow the same advice.

Get the Real Thing.

BUILDING contractors are known for taking short-cuts. A favorite: substituting poorer quality parts and materials and charging you for top-of-the-line goods. Before signing an agreement, tell the contractor that you want receipts for all materials. Go over them carefully and call the distributor or manufacturer directly regarding anything questionable.

Buy at the End of a Cruise.

PRICES IN the onboard gift shops drop dramatically the closer the ship get to the shore. Look for up to 50% off.

Fix Up Tax Mistakes.

IF YOU MADE an error, amend your return ASAP, before the IRS catches it, and you'll avoid hefty negligence penalties. It's your responsibility to right the wrong, even if an employer or your accountant made the initial goof. File Form 1040X, available by calling the IRS at 800–829–3676.

Pamper Your Pet and Your Purse.

SAVE **30% TO 75%** on Fido's food and Kitty's supplies by order-ing from a mail order discounter. Try: The Pet Warehouse, 800–443–1160; or Doctors Foster & Smith, 800–826–7206.

– ¢ –

Keep Your Luggage out of Sight.

IF YOU WANT to negotiate a hotel or motel discount, don't lug your heavy bags, backpacks and steamer trunks into the lobby. That makes it pretty obvious you're not going anywhere else.

Never Book a Hotel Through Its Toll-Free Number.

AT LEAST NOT until you've called the hotel directly. The manager there, not the operator, decides when to reduce room rates—after 6 P.M., on weekends, when the hotel isn't busy.

— ¢ —

Make Buying Mutual Funds Simple.

GET THEM through a single source with a number of choices, such as Charles Schwab's OneSource, (800–435–4000) or Fidelity's Funds Network (800–544–9697).

Get New Money from Old Tax Returns.

IF YOU OR your accountant discover a missed opportunity you can amend your return within three years after filing. Use IRS Form 1040X. Reasons: a 1099 that came in late or was inaccurate; misplaced records for business expenses or charitable contributions, casualty loss in a presidentially declared disaster area and retroactive changes in the tax code.

Smile When You Turn 65.

NOW YOU CAN collect full Social Security benefits. Had you taken benefits at 62 your check would be significantly less, forever.

— ¢ —

Get the Family Together on the Cheap.

FAMILY REUNIONS don't have to be expensive. Check out local, state and national parks. If you want to meet in a centrally located place, the nonprofit group American Youth Hostels (202–783–6161) has interesting, inexpensive places—mansions, farm houses, lighthouses, log cabins in every single state.

Protect Yourself with Prepaid Phone Cards.

THEY HAVE A cap on how much can be charged. If they're lost or stolen, you're out only that amount. But lose your long distance carrier credit card, your financial exposure at maximum may be unlimited; at minimum, a headache to fix.

— ¢ —

Send Your New Broker Your Old Statement.

DO THIS BEFORE officially transferring your account. It helps your new advisor to know what assets to expect and, if anything's missing, you'll both be able to tell.

Hire an Expert.

NOTHING IS MORE stressful in life than trying to be who you are not, trying to do what you cannot. If you hate managing your money, don't. Instead, find someone who'd like to do it for you. It's worth a fee or commission to get a first-rate pro.

Don't Borrow from Your 401(K) If You're Thinking of Changing Jobs.

IF YOU DO, you must repay your loan in full before moving on. Most employers give only 60 to 90 days to come up with the cash. Otherwise, the loan becomes a distribution and you'll owe taxes on the amount outstanding. And, if you're under age 59½ you'll also be hit with a 10% IRS penalty.

Don't Be a Dummy: Graduate.

ACCORDING TO the Bureau of Labor Statistics, since 1976, high school grads' real earnings have fallen 10% while college grads have had gains of 6%. And, year after year, college grads land an average 16% more of the jobs in all industries than workers with only high school diplomas.

Get Out of Your Car Lease Early.

IF YOU NO longer need the vehicle, find someone with a good credit record to take over your lease; you'll have to pay a small amount for the transfer and surrender, but it will be worth it.

$TIP: This works best with a large, major car dealer; they're much more flexible than those that deal with only a handful of leases each year.

Write a Will.

EVEN IF YOU THINK you don't have a fortune. You undoubtedly have more than you realize—a camera, a VCR, a CD player, computer, a printer, a car, nice clothes, some jewelry, perhaps a house or even two. If you die without a will or a living trust, all your worldly possessions will be distributed according to state law. States generally give one-third to one-half of your after-tax estate to your surviving spouse and the rest to your kids. If you have neither a spouse nor kids, then it goes to your parents, brothers and sisters and other blood relatives. If you have no living relatives, then the state gets it. And to add insult to injury, your estate will have to pay a court–appointed outsider for managing the whole affair.

— ¢ —

Read the Small Print.

CREDIT CARD ISSUERS have the right to raise rates if they give cardholders 15 days' notice. If your rate goes up, call the issuer and negotiate for a lower one; threaten to walk if they balk.

Rent from a Car Dealer.

NEW CAR WARRANTIES often require dealers to pay for a rental car when an owner's car is in for repairs. Many dealers find it cheaper to rent out their own cars. Call several in your area before heading for a traditional rental agency. Chrysler, Ford and Toyota have the largest rental programs.

Send Your New Broker Your Old Statement.

DO THIS BEFORE officially transferring your account. It helps your new advisor to know what assets to expect and, if anything's missing, you'll both be able to tell.

Peek at Your Mutuals Just Twice a Year.

IF YOU LOOK at your mutual fund's performance more than that you'll be tempted to trade unnecessarily—perhaps because its performance has slipped slightly or you've heard about some new hot fund. This is a mistake. Most funds are designed to be long-term investments. Hold stock funds at least five years and bond funds at least three. EXCEPTION: Sector and aggressive funds.

Bring Your Own Shampoo to the Hospital.

MARKUP ON toiletries, cosmetics, pajamas, bathrobes, slippers, special pillows, deodorants and lotions can be as much as 100% when delivered to your room.

— ¢ —

Be Smarter.

If the deal sounds too good to be true, it probably is.

Budget For Mistakes.

DON'T BE TOO hard on yourself if you pick the wrong mutual fund, pay too much for an airline ticket, misjudge the stock market. Allot for errors in your annual or monthly budget. And then, pick up the pieces and move on, taking comfort from the adage, "Behold the turtle; he makes progress only when he sticks his neck out."

Get a Loan Approved When You Don't Need It.

BANKS PREFER TO lend money to the nondesperate, which means it's tough to get a home equity or business loan if you're out of work or are dealing with some type of disaster. Start the time-consuming paperwork well in advance of any anticipated need. If you never need the money, so much the better.

Write One Check for Both Parents.

IF YOU'RE PROVIDING most of their support and they file separate returns, write checks to just one. The IRS says you must provide more than half of a relative's support in order to get the exemption. Don't divide the money, which only makes it harder to satisfy the ruling.

Know Your Retirement Rights.

WIVES ARE guaranteed to receive a part of their husband's pension if their husband dies first—unless they've signed away that right. Sometimes couples opt to receive a "single lifetime" payout because it gives them more income than the "joint and survivor" choice. **CAUTION:** With the single lifetime choice, benefits stop when the husband dies.

Find Lost Money.

EACH STATE and the District of Columbia has an office of unclaimed property. Contact yours to locate dormant bank accounts, old insurance policies, utility deposits, uncashed government checks. Click on: www.unclaimedassets.com.

— ¢ —

Be Very Blasé.

WHEN SHOPPING at flea markets, garage sales, antique shops, or anywhere else where bargaining is de rigueur.

Bump Up Your Homeowners' Insurance.

IF CONSUMER PRICES start to rise and your policy does not have an inflation escalator clause, you'll need to add coverage to adjust for increased replacement costs of such items as furniture, appliances and valuables, as well as for the house itself.

Cut Yakkity-Yak.

IF YOU STRUGGLE to keep your phone bills in line, use prepaid phone cards. They have a limit on how much can be charged to them. When it's used up, you have to hang up.

Clean the Tires.

YOU'LL GET 10% to 15% more for your used car if the inside and outside are shiny and sparkling. Reason: the car dealer will know you've taken great care of the vehicle, including under the hood. Use Armor All, Windex and Turbo Wax on all the right places. Wipe, but don't steam-clean, the engine.

Avoid Being Taxed Twice.

IF YOU BORROW from your 401(k) plan, you are borrowing pre-tax dollars but paying the money back with after-tax dollars. That means when you retire and start withdrawing the money, you'll pay tax a second time on the loan that you repaid.

— ¢ —

Use a Hotel Consolidator.

THEY BUY rooms in bulk in all major cities and then sell them at a discount to the public. Call: QUIKBOOK (800–789–9887) and HOTEL RESERVATION NETWORK (800–964–6835).

Make a Contract with Your Contractor.

HOME IMPROVEMENTS are full of traps and horror stories. Before hiring a contractor, visit sites he's worked on, check with your city or state building agencies to make sure his license is valid and that he has $100,000 to $300,000 in liability insurance. Then, when he presents you with an estimate, put down only 10%. Pay the rest in four stages, holding the final 10% until 10 days after the project is finished to your satisfaction.

Join the Wives and Collect Social Security.

IF YOU WERE married for at least ten years, and have not remarried, you can collect benefits when you turn 62, based on your ex-husband's earnings, even if he's remarried. If you're his current wife, you too can collect benefits at 62.

Take a Profit.

NO ONE EVER lost money by selling their investments for more than they paid for them.

Avoid Probate.

IT COSTS 5% to 10% of an estate's assets to distribute them. And it's time–consuming. Instead, set up POD (Payable-on-Death) bank accounts, in which you name a beneficiary for whatever is left in your bank account after you die. There's no fee involved and you can change the beneficiary as often as you like. Do the same for your retirement accounts and, if your state permits it, for your securities and your car. But check with your lawyer or accountant first.

Protect Your 401(K) Plan.

SIGNS OF FRAUD: your quarterly statement is always late; your payroll deductions don't match the contributions shown on the statement; your account drops in value and it can't be explained by the market; people who've left the company have problems collecting benefits.

$TIP: Talk with your firm's benefits officer. If you hit a blank wall, call the Federal Pension & Welfare Benefits Administration at: 202–219–8776.

Use Your House, Not Pension, as Equity

IF YOU ARE strapped for cash, a home-equity loan is usually better choice, if you itemize deductions. Interest is deductible, whereas interest on a 401(k) loan is not.

Find the Light.

BEFORE BUYING anything indoors, take it outdoors or at least to a window. Fabrics, colors, finishes all change in the sunshine. This is also the best way to detect scratches, chips, runs, flaws—and if you do, negotiate a discount, in broad daylight.

Don't Confuse Joint with Common.

PROPERTY HELD AS joint tenants means each tenant has an equal right to the entire property. If it is joint tenancy with rights of survivorship, then the surviving partner automatically owns the whole property when the other one dies. Tenants in common, on the other hand, means each partner owns a share of the property; it can be equal or unequal shares. When one dies, his or her interest passes to the person named in his or her will or living trust—that may or may not be the partner with whom the property was owned.

Know Your A, B, C's.

MUTUAL FUNDS with "B" shares have back-end loads or fees—which means you pay a fee when you sell. Funds with "A" shares require a fee going in, when you buy shares. Be smart: Don't go into a fund without knowing all the fees involved.

Shop Alone.

WHEN A CHILD, spouse, best friend or parent tags along, you always seem to wind up spending more than you intended.

Take Good Care of Fido

IN MOST STATES, you cannot leave a pet money or property in your will; if you do, it simply becomes part of your estate and goes to your other beneficiaries. So, make arrangements to give Kitty to someone who loves her as much as you do and leave money in your will for that person, with the understanding it's to cover the pet's expenses.

Start an Education IRA for Your Child.

THE MAXIMUM contribution is only $500/year, but begin in year one and fund it annually for 17 years and you'll have about $25,000 when baby turns 18, assuming the account earns 10% annually. The money can be withdrawn tax free if used to pay for tuition, fees and books for graduate or undergraduate education.

$TIP: Contributors need not be parents or even relatives.

Insure for a Very Long Life.

NEVER BUY a long-term health care policy that doesn't have inflation protection. If you live long enough to use it, the cost of living will certainly have gone up. As W.C. Fields was fond of saying regarding inflation: "The cost of living has gone up another dollar a quart."

Deduct Interest on Student Loans.

IF YOU TAKE out a commercial or federally backed loan, such as a Stafford or Perkins loan, be sure to deduct the interest. The max in 1999 is $1,500; that rises to $2,000 in 2000 and $2,500 in 2001. You're entitled to this tax break whether or not you itemize on your federal tax return.

Protect Your Child.

IF YOUR SPOUSE is a deadbeat parent and owes child support, you should know that the new Child Support Law makes crossing a state line to avoid paying a felony, subject to two years in prison. For help in finding a missing parent, get in touch with the Association for Children Enforcement Services (ACES) in Toledo, OH at: 800–537–7072.

Make a Big Fuss About Fees.

ACCORDING to the U.S. Department of Labor, many companies overcharge their employees when it comes to administering their 401(k) plans. To find out if your company is one of the bad guys, get a free copy of "A Look at 401(k) Plan Fees" by calling 800–998–7542 or click on: www.dol.gov/dol/pwba/.

— ¢ —

Mind Your Manners.

IF YOU DECIDE to change your accountant, stockbroker, financial planner, lawyer or real estate agent, be very nice about it. You may need to ask your old advisor for copies of tax returns, confirmation slips or other key documents. And, sometimes the grass seems greener on the other side of the desk. You may decide to go back to where you were.

Sidestep Hotel Bills.

SWAP YOUR house or apartment with someone else's for your next vacation—in this country or abroad—and you'll eliminate the most expensive component of a holiday. List your house at least six months in advance with a leading service, such as: World Wide Travel Exchange, 800–549–9076 or click on: wwte.com.

Get a Q-Tip.

PROTECT YOUR spouse and your kids at the same time by setting up a QUALIFIED TERMINABLE INTEREST PROPERTY Trust, affectionately known as a Q-TIP. This way, all of the income generated by the assets in the trust will go to the surviving spouse for life. But you are the one who determines how these assets will be distributed after your spouse's death. If you've remarried, this is one way to make sure your children from an earlier marriage inherit some or all of your money.

Go for the GAP.

INSURANCE THAT IS, not clothes. If you lease a car, GAP insurance guarantees the difference or the gap between what you would collect from an insurance company in case of theft or an accident and what you might get from the leasing company. Leasing is a tricky business. Read the Federal Trade Commission's consumer publication, "Keys to Vehicle Leasing" at: www.ftc.gov.

Have HOPE.

DON'T OVERLOOK the new HOPE scholarship tax credit when filing your 1040. It's worth up to $1,500 for the cost of the first two years of post-secondary school incurred by you, your spouse or your child. The credit equals 100% of the first $1,000 of expenses and 50% of the next $1,000 of expenses, per tax year.

Don't Put Your Will in a Safe Deposit Box.

ONLY A COPY; ditto your health care proxy, life insurance policy or other documents your heirs would need in an emergency. Very often boxes are sealed when the owner dies.

Take The 10% Solution.

BUY STOCKS of companies that have increased their dividends 10% a year for 10 years, such as Student Loan Marketing Association (Sallie Mae) and Federal National Mortgage Association (Fannie Mae). Ask your broker for others.

Get a Copy of Your Stockbroker's Report Card.

YOU CAN RUN a check on any broker's disciplinary record. Hopefully yours won't have one, but to make sure get in touch with the National Association of Securities Dealers at 800–289–9999 or click on: www.nasdr.com.

Learn for a Lifetime.

THE NEW Lifetime Learning Credit equals 20% of up to $5,000 of the cost of any instruction at an educational institution that enables you to acquire or improve a job skill. Both undergrad and grad school instruction qualify for the tax credit. Check with your accountant about limitations.

A Heads Up for Adopting Parents.

THERE'S A onetime federal tax credit of up to $5,000 for each child you adopt ($6,000 for a child with "special needs"). The credit, for expenses such as the adoption itself, attorney's fees, court costs, even travel, is deducted directly from taxes you owe.

$TIP: Keep all canceled checks and related documents.

Use Your Age.

WHEN DECIDING how much to invest in fixed-income securities, such as bonds, CDs, Treasuries and money market funds, the rule of thumb is—go by your age. If you're 40, no more than 40% should be in these investments. Put the rest in stocks.

Track the Trailer Time Line.

IF YOU'RE thinking of buying a manufactured home, make sure it was built after 1974 when the HUD building code started mandating exactly how homes were anchored to the ground; after 1994 is even better as the code added wind standards. Details: Manufactured Housing Institute, 703–558–0400 or click on: www.mfghome.org.

Insist on an Itemized Bill.

ACCORDING TO Consumers Union, more than 50% of hospital bills contain mistakes. Read yours, question anything you don't understand and look for double charges. One out of two bills is revised in favor of the patient—but only if you speak up.

Retire Your Mortgage Long Before You Do.

YOU WANT TO MAKE payments when you're on a fixed income?

Don't Rush Out of Town.

MANY RETIREES immediately dash to Florida, Arizona or other warm–weather havens only to discover six months later that they are too far away from family and friends and life is not as wonderful as they expected.

$TIP: Rent for six months before going to the trouble and expense of selling your house and moving. Do it during the summer so you'll know if you can stand the heat in the kitchen.

Make Extra Money.

BE A TRADE show rep (contact your convention and visitors bureau for a list of upcoming conventions); read for the vision impaired (contact nursing homes, hospitals, seniors' groups); make and deliver meals to busy families; clip for a local newspaper clipping bureau; take care of other people's pets and plants, tutor or coach people in your area of expertise.

$TIP: Freelance income entitles you to open a Keogh or SEP retirement plan.

Toss the Dog a Bone.

INVESTING IN the "Dogs of the Dow" over the past ten years has beaten the performance of 99% of all actively managed mutual funds. The dogs are the ten Dow Jones Industrial Average stocks with the highest yields. Adjust your portfolio once a year, at the same time—perhaps on your birthday.

$TIP: The *Wall Street Journal* lists the 30 Dow industrials each day; check the yield for each one.

Document Your Kindness.

IF YOU CLAIM a charitable tax deduction for gifts of used items worth $250 or more, it must be substantiated by a signed receipt written on the charity's letterhead. If your largesse totals more than $500, fill out Form 8283, "Noncash Charitable Organizations," listing which method you used to value your donation—snapshots help.

$TIP: Donations over $1,500 catch the attention of the IRS. If you made large donations because you moved, say so.

Donate Your Car to Charity.

AND GET A tax deduction for its fair market value. If it's an old clunker and doesn't run, it can be sold for parts. The National Kidney Foundation will even pick it up, unless the car is on an island in the ocean. Call: 800–488–2277.

Sell Your Home on the Range.

YOU'LL MOVE your house faster if you put it on the market with a price range rather than listing just one figure. This gives buyers the message that you're serious and will consider reasonable offers.

Know Your Hospital's Check-In and Checkout Times.

IF YOU ARRIVE too early or stay too late, you'll be charged for an extra day.

Follow Your Heart.

WHEN YOU get married, review your 401(k), IRA, insurance policies and will. Chances are when you were just starting out you named your parents and/or siblings as your beneficiaries. Update now to include your spouse. Ditto if you divorce or re-marry—that is, bring your beneficiary up to speed.

Don't Send Granny to Jail.

CONGRESS eliminated criminal penalties for nursing home patients who disposed of their assets illegally in order to qualify for coverage under Medicaid. But unless you're the one in the nursing home, be careful. Any paid advisor, such as a lawyer, accountant or financial planner, who gives advice that results in illegal disposal of assets is still subject to criminal penalties. Talk with an certified Elder Care lawyer first for the best advice. To find one, contact the National Academy of Elder Law Attorneys, 520-881-4005 or click on: www.naela.com.

Look Under the Mattress.

AS PRESIDENT Roosevelt said in 1933, "It is safer to keep your money in a reopened bank than under your mattress." You can do one better by putting your stashed cash in a money market fund. Rates are 1 to 3% higher than in a bank account. Just about every mutual fund family has a money market fund with free checking.

Make It SIMPLE.

IF YOU HAVE a small business and want to provide retirement benefits for your workers, look into a SIMPLE retirement plan. There's very little paperwork and eligible employees—those paid at least $5,000 a year for the current and two preceding years—may contribute up to $6,000/year through salary deduction. Details: Pension & Welfare Benefits Administration, 800–998–7542 or click on: www.dol.gov.

Get Your HMO to Pay, or Turn "No" Into "Yes."

IF AFTER CALLING and writing your HMO, payment for your treatment is still denied, ask your doctor to write a letter to the company on your behalf. Then get in touch with your state insurance commission and let the HMO know you're going outside the plan to fight the rejection. For heavy duty support, contact the Center for Patient Advocacy at 800–846–7444 or click on: www.patientadvocacy.org.

Barter Better.

TRADE WHAT you do well—repairing computers, fixing old cars, baking pies—with something someone else does—tax returns, cabinetmaking, landscaping. But, barter with someone you know, get the terms (who, what, when and how) in writing and to avoid running afoul of the IRS, report the value of the goods or services you received on Line 21, "Other Income" on your Form 1040.

— ¢ —

Check Out Prices.

DON'T BUY A thing until you compare offerings from different manufacturers through: www.compare.net. It has a database of 10,000+ models of products in 40+ categories, from cars, cameras and cell phones to trucks, TVs and toaster ovens. And be sure to check out a product's performance and reliability with *Consumer Reports* magazine at: www.ConsumerReports.org.

Buy Where the Contractors Buy.

BEFORE YOU purchase another home renovation item, get the mail order catalog from Maintenance Warehouse, a subsidiary of Home Depot, at 800-431-3000. It has thousands of items in stock, ready for free next day delivery. If you're unhappy with your lighting fixture or new bathtub, they'll make it right. Among the items available: plumbing supplies, hardware, appliances, tools, telephones, paint, flashlights, batteries, screens, locks. Prices are incredibly low.

Stick with Your Mutual Fund.

IF THE MANAGER leaves, don't immediately dash out the door if the fund has been a strong performer. New managers generally hold the same stocks for several months and follow the previous manager's investment strategies for up to a year. Switch out only when total return figures drop several months in a row.

Crawl Out from Under.

IF YOU'RE REALLY drowning in debt get help, but only from a nonprofit organization such as the National Foundation for Consumer Credit (800–682–9832 or click on: www.nfcc.org). It helps families and individuals take control of their finances, pay off credit card debt and set up sound budgets. Avoid for-profit groups that charge expensive fees. Most are real rip-offs.

Fill Up the Tank.

IF YOU HEAR that a severe storm, flooding or fires are headed your way, gas the car immediately. A power outage often makes it impossible for gas stations to pump fuel. Keep the automatic garage door control off and move your car into the driveway.

— ¢ —

Follow the Leader.

IF TOP–LEVEL executives are selling shares in their corporation or if management as a whole owns only 10% or less, they obviously don't think too highly of the company. Nor should you.

Get Mortgage Approval Before Picking Out the House.

As BOB HOPE remarked, "A bank is a place that will lend you money if you can prove you don't need it." Once you have your loan approval, aim to spend less.

Don't Always Be in Hot Water

ADD A programmable time control unit to your hot water tank. You'll save 20% in energy costs.

Cash In Your EE Savings Bonds.

AFTER THESE bonds mature, they no longer earn interest. Either roll them over into HH Savings Bonds (which earn 4%) or get your money back. To find the redemption value of older bonds, click on: www.publicdebt.treas.gov or call the Department of Treasury at: 202–377–7715 and press option #5.

Get Help from FREDDIE & FANNIE.

IF YOU DON'T have enough money for a down payment on a house, Freddie Mac, a government-sponsored company, has special programs for low– and middle–income buyers with very little cash. Check with your local bank or mortgage broker. Fannie Mae has similar loans: 800–732–6643 or click on: www.homepath.com.

— ¢ —

Trade Down and Down and Down.

WANT TO SELL the old family home for a smaller one but reluctant to do so because of the capital gains tax? The new law makes it easier. It repealed the rollover and age provisions and increased the excluded amount to $250,000 for an individual and $500,000 for a married couple, provided you've lived in the home for at least two of the past five years.

$TIP: You can use the exclusion as often as every two years.

Buy Buybacks.

A CORPORATION that buys back its own shares is saying it has confidence in the company. It also indicates there's enough cash on hand to do so. Not surprisingly, shares tend to rise on the announcement, with further demand created as the program is implemented. Buybacks also reduce the number of shares outstanding, which in turn increases earnings per share.

Mistakes Happen.

TRY TO FIGURE out why, vow not to do it again and move on. Even hotshot Wall Street pros make errors. As Oscar Wilde said, "Experience is the name everyone gives to their mistakes."

Brown Bag It.

TAKE YOUR LUNCH to work. Do it three days a week at $7/lunch and you'll have saved $1,008 in a year—use it to cut your credit card debt.

Find Your Money.

WHEN WILLIE SUTTON was asked why he robbed banks he said: "That's where the money is." You should know where yours is, too—your checking and savings accounts, CDs, mutual funds and brokerage accounts. If you've got more than five, consider consolidating or at least keep a current list and give a copy to your lawyer, accountant or spouse.

Get Separate Home Office Insurance.

MOST HOMEOWNERS' policies cover only up to $2,500 in equipment—the cost of an upscale computer and color printer. SOLUTION: Buy a rider to make up the difference. Or, if your annual revenues are over $35,000, get a separate business policy. It will protect accounts receivable, inventory, business disruption losses and other items.

Think Big.

DON'T WORRY about finding every single penny. You'll either drive yourself crazy or get bored with the whole budgeting process. Instead, focus on where the dollars are going, keeping in mind the comforting words of Robert Frost:

> Never Ask of Money Spent
> Where The Spender Thinks It Went
> Nobody Was Ever Meant
> To Remember or Invent
> What He Did With Every Cent.

Buy Lawn Furniture and Barbeque Grills in September.

DITTO FOR OUTDOOR cooking utensils and portable heaters.

— ¢ —

Dump Credit Card Debt.

IF YOU CARRY a $3,000 credit card balance (typical for many Americans) and the rate is 18%, it will cost you at least $540 a year in interest. Need we say more?

Demand Performance.

LET YOUR financial advisors know you expect them to do a first-rate job for you. And reward them when they do—by a written letter of praise with a copy to their boss plus lunch or dinner at his or her favorite restaurant, with you picking up the (tax-deductible) bill. A "ho-hum" attitude on your part will get "ho-hum" results.

Roll in the Right Direction.

IF YOU'RE changing jobs, transfer your 401(k) into a rollover IRA at a major mutual fund family or a discount broker. You'll have many more investments to choose from than if you leave your money with your former employer or transfer it to you new employer's plan. Setting up a rollover IRA is both tax and penalty free, PROVIDED the money is transferred from institution to institution and not by you personally.

Dance Your Way on Board.

IF YOU'RE A NICE, polite gentleman who knows more than the box step, you may very well qualify for a free cruise. Cruise lines regularly seek out men to dance with unattached women sailing the high seas. Call your favorite ship.

Don't Bet on Your Bets.

LOSSES AT THE gambling table or racetrack are deductible from your winnings, but only up to the amount you win...and losses cannot be deducted from any other forms of income. So, to deduct $5,000 in bad bets, you must have $5,000 in winnings. And if you win $5,000 or more in the lottery, your winnings are subject to withholdings of 28%. Maybe you should stay home or at least keep in mind a veteran gambler's adage: "Never bet on anything that eats more than you do."

Buy Things You Long for at Government Auctions.

PROPERTY SEIZED by the Drug Enforcement Administration, the Justice Department and the FBI goes up for auction on a regular basis. Save big bucks on toys that kingpins and drug lords like to sport: big cars, big houses, big planes, big boats, big motorcycles. For "The National List of Authorized Sellers of Forfeited Property," call the Federal Information Center at 800–688–8989.

Know What the IRS Knows.

A NEW REGULATION allows banks to contact the IRS if you're behind six months or more in credit card or other payments. If the bank notifies the IRS it will also send you a 1099-C tax form, which requires you to report the unpaid debt as income and pay taxes on it. Ignore it and the IRS will chase you.

$TIP: If you fall behind, don't hide. Call your lenders to work out extended terms. They won't yell at you; in fact, they'll be happy to hear from you.

Know How Far You Can Drive.

MANY CAR LEASES won't let you take the vehicle out of your state for longer than 30 days at a time. Violate this and you could be hit with a big penalty. Before signing the contract, get this restriction removed if you plan on being away from home.

Bounce Along with the Baby Boomers.

FOLLOW WHAT they need and like. These are the areas of investment growth for the next five to ten years. That means companies in these industries: drugs and pharmaceuticals, financial services, retirement living, computers, discount stores, travel.

Bend Your Knees When Shopping.

THE HIGHEST priced items in grocery and drug stores are always at eye level.

Stop Smoking and Tell Everyone.

Especially your life insurance agent. Most policies have lower rates for nonsmokers. Typically, the annual premium will drop from about $650 to $300 for a 40-year-old man with a $250,000 policy who hasn't smoked in a year. But, don't lie. Should you die within the first few years after declaring yourself nicotine-free, there will be an investigation and your beneficiary may not get full benefits.

Dump Index Funds in a Tricky Market.

WHEN STOCKS are overpriced, in trouble or fall out of favor, managers of growth funds sell their shares. With an index fund, however, they cannot sell, but must hold whatever stocks are in the index, which gives little protection when the Dow is jumpy.

Carry a Memo Pad.

ELECTRONIC OR spiral. Jot everything down. Good financial advice, particularly involving unfamiliar companies, new terminology or strange concepts, disappears like ice cubes in the sun.

Piggyback Your Mortgage.

THE NEW piggyback loan is a small second mortgage covering the gap between your down payment and the 20% the lender requires. It's a better deal than Private Mortgage Insurance (PMI), required when you don't have the 20%, because interest payments on the piggyback are tax deductible while PMI premiums are not.

Call Your Kid's College if You're Having Money Problems.

IF YOUR financial situation takes a turn for the worse—you or your spouse have been downsized or you've had to take a new job at a lower salary–explain the specifics in a letter to the financial aid office. Your student will get more help.

Start Small.

TEST CONTRACTORS, office help, maids, baby–sitters, housekeepers, accountants, lawyers and others by using them for small jobs or limited hours. Try several before selecting one to handle major or long–term assignments. Mistakes are expensive.

— ¢ —

Beat Those ATM Surcharges.

USE MACHINES sponsored by members of No-Surcharge ATM Alliance, which includes 300+ credit unions and 120+ U.S. banks. Info: 888–748–3266 or click on: www.theco-op.org.

Test Drive a Cold Engine.

WHEN PICKING out a car, sport utility vehicle or truck, make sure the seller has not warmed up the car. Then while it idles, get out and take a look at the tailpipe. If there's black smoke (a problem with the fuel system), blue smoke (burning oil) or white smoke (coolant seeping into the cylinders), says thanks but no thanks.

Happy Camper Savings.

THERE ARE unadvertised discounts for those who speak up and ask: when more than one kid in the family attends camp at the same time, for early enrollment, for the less popular second session and for bringing in a full paying camper. Nonprofit camps are at least 50% less expensive than private ones. Check with the YMCA, YWCA, Boy and Girl Scouts, B'nai B'rith and your local church or synagogue.

Tell It to the IRS.

IF YOU ARE claiming large deductions or other unusual items on your tax return, add clearly typed explanations. You'll reduce the risk of an audit, provided your explanation is honest and the deduction legitimate. Examples: setting up a home office resulting in business expenses; large charitable contributions resulting from the death of a family member or a move; an adult child leaving home or a new job search.

Little and Big Things Matter in Home Improvements.

KEEP RECORDS of all improvements so you can add them to your home's basis and reduce your taxes when you sell. You can include the cost of any item if it improves the home and you can't take it with you when you move. Examples: a new room, garage, swimming pool, deck, built-in bookcases, ceiling fans, cabinets, wall-to-wall carpeting, fences, storm windows, alarm system, landscaping.

Buy in Multiples.

IF YOU GIVE presents to many people, buy in bulk and negotiate a discount. Unisex choices: scarves, gloves, picture frames, photo albums, wine, cheese and crackers, gourmet goodies, candy, paperweights, letter openers and plants.

— ¢ —

Don't Insure the Kids.

IT'S INEXPENSIVE, and the purpose of insurance is to leave money after the insured person dies. Your kids are financially dependent on you so it's you who needs coverage for them.

Cut Insomnia.

FOR MOST OF us, mutual fund prospectuses are a big yawn. Yet there are only four points you must look for and it will take just ten minutes. 1) THE TOTAL RETURN FIGURES, year by year. 2) YEARLY DISTRIBUTION OF CAPITAL GAINS. Lots of trading means higher taxes for you. 3) ANNUAL EXPENSES. Also listed in the "Financial Highlights" table. With a U.S. stock fund, no higher than 1.4%. 4) INVESTMENT PHILOSOPHY. If it is vague or unclear, find another fund.

Follow Knowledge, Not Hunches.

DON'T MAKE financial decisions based on guesswork, rumors and emotions. Gather the facts. Study the facts. Discuss the facts with a professional. Then make your move. Stocks, bonds, CDs, savings accounts, gold, silver and real estate do not have feelings.

Sell Your Mutual Fund.

IF IT LAGS its peer group for 12 months or more. When new sales charges are added. When management continually changes. When it closes its doors to new investors *and* its performance declines.

— ¢ —

Work Out at a School.

HEALTH CLUBS, especially in cities, are pricey. Check out your alma mater or nearby college, university or prep school. Most let alumni and/or neighbors use the facilities for nominal fees.

Pay for the Small Stuff.

MINIMIZE the number of insignificant claims you file on your auto and home insurance. Companies are more likely to cancel policies or raise premiums when people file several small claims—but not if they file one large one. Insurance is intended to help you recover from a disaster, not every little problem. But, always file if there's a possibility of personal injury, either to you or someone else.

— ¢ —

Restructure Rather Than Refinance Your Mortgage.

MANY LENDERS have set up programs to keep current customers from straying. Restructuring, which is really refinancing with your present lender, will get you a lower interest rate as well as reduced transaction fees.

"All-Risk" Is Risky.

SO-CALLED ALL-RISK homeowners' insurance protects from "all risks"—unless, that is, they are excluded by the policy. Examples: flood/lightning damage, water seepage, sewers. Ask.

— ¢ —

Call AMTRAK in the Wee Small Hours.

IF YOU WANT to get on a sold-out car, especially a sleeper. Space opens up after midnight when the computerized system knocks out reservations that haven't been paid for by the duedate.

Donate Appreciated Securities to Your Favorite Charity Instead of Cash.

THIS GIVES the charity the full value of the shares and you their full value as a deduction. Sell your shares to raise cash, and you have to pay capital gains on the profit. For example, if shares you bought for $2,000 are now worth $5,000, you'd have to pay tax on the $3,000 profit. Give them to the charity and you'll get a $5,000 deduction.

Know the Difference Between a Credit and a Deduction.

A TAX DEDUCTION reduces your taxable income; mortgage interest and charitable donations are tax deductible. If you're in the 28% tax bracket, then every $100 deduction cuts your taxes by $28. A tax CREDIT is more valuable because it's a dollar-for-dollar write-off against the taxes you owe. Credits include: child and/or dependent care; for the elderly or disabled; for taxes paid to other countries; HOPE and Lifetime Learning credits.

Loyalty Does Count.

MANUFACTURERS, companies, small firms and many restaurants reward longtime customers. But it's up to you to let them know how long you've been a member of the faithful. For example, Chrysler, Ford and GM give loyalty-discount coupons worth $500 to $1,000 to original owners of one of their cars made since 1986.

Make Biweekly Mortgage Payments.

ON A $100,000 loan at 8.2%, monthly payments are about $740. Biweekly payments of $383 retires the loan in 21 years instead of 30. Your interest will be $110,888, or $64,354 less.

—¢—

Put a Timer Next to the Phone.

SET IT FOR as long as you think you should talk, not as long as you wish to talk. When it goes off, it's time for you to get off.

The Older the Better.

IF YOU WAIT beyond age 65 to collect Social Security, you'll earn delayed-retirement credits. That means every check will be larger than it would have been had you started collecting at the normal age of 65. For those born in 1931 or 1932, the credit is 5% for each year benefits are delayed, up to age 70. The credit rises until it peaks at 8% for people born in 1943 or later.

Never Say You're Sorry.

WHEN YOU HAVE an auto accident of any kind. It will be used later on as proof that you admitted responsibility. Instead, give only your name, address and car registration information to the other driver, to anyone injured and to the police at the scene. Get the same information from the other people involved as well as the names and addresses of witnesses and the police officer's name and badge number. Then keep quiet until you talk with your insurance agent and your lawyer.

Sell a Mutual Fund When Its Expenses Have Become too High.

COMPARE IT with these "Morningstar" averages: U.S. stock funds (1.42%); small cap (1.50%); mid-cap (1.56%); large cap (1.27%); foreign stock funds (1.67%); emerging markets (2.06%); government bond funds (1.06%); municipal bond funds (0.92%); and corporate bond funds (0.95%).

— ¢ —

Get a Discount from a Full Service Broker.

THEY KNOW competition is tough, not only from discount brokers but now from on-line services. None of them volunteer discounts, but ask, especially if you have a balance over $200,000, trade frequently, have been a longtime customer, have a young or new broker who wants your business or if you're a relative.

Never Balance Your Checkbook on Tuesday.

IF YOU DEPOSIT your paycheck on Friday, it may not have cleared by Tuesday. Bills you paid and mailed over the weekend will take at least until Wednesday to clear. So on Tuesday, read the other book in this series: NEVER CALL YOUR BROKER ON MONDAY AND 300 OTHER FINANCIAL LESSONS YOU CAN'T AFFORD NOT TO KNOW!